POINT LOBOS

AN ILLUSTRATED WALKER'S HANDBOOK

BY FRANCES THOMPSON

FOREWORD BY JUDSON VANDEVERE

PUBLISHED IN COOPERATION WITH THE
POINT LOBOS NATURAL HISTORY ASSC.

inkstone

published by

Inkstone Books
Box 172 Carmel
California, 93923

first printing December, 1980

Library of Congress Catalog Card Number: 80-82176
ISBN: 0-9604542-0-9

printed in the United States of America

CONTENTS

FOREWORD

Point Lobos Reserve is the crown jewel of California's State Park system. And, in my opinion, Frances Thompson's <u>Point Lobos</u>, <u>An Illustrated Walker's Handbook</u> is an outstanding artistic and descriptive representation of this most precious headland. Her masterful views of each trail, which represent their breathtaking natural features, are a most pleasing and unique method of interpretation. Frances' love for the beauty of wild things is apparent in each charming view. This fine work is especially appealing to me, for I had the pleasure of assisting Reserve visitors during the eight summers of my service as a Seasonal Naturalist.

In addition to the visual pleasures which this Handbook so beautifully complements; the full Point Lobos experience is one of sounds: wind and waves, chickadees and oyster-catchers; one of odors: aromatic scrubs and drying seaweeds, yerba buena and skunk weed; one of textures: common and leather stars, granodiorite and rhyolite; one of tastes: sea staghorn and old-ladies-chewing-tobacco; one of temperatures: hot south-facing midden-covered slopes and cool north-facing bluff-lettuce hung slopes; one of humidity: bursting seed pods along dusty trails and fog-dripping cypresses; one of movement: rush of wind through contorted trees and crashing surf against eroding terraces; one of seasons: riotous blooms and blowing pappus; one of varied topography: Big Dome and Carmel Submarine Canyon, towering pines and understory oaks; and one of tides: life-giving spray to periwinkles and foraging opportunities for shore birds.

Judson Vandevere

Monterey, California
October 1980

ABOUT THE BOOK

Welcome. You are beginning a tour around Point Lobos State Reserve. This book is to assist you if you'd like to know something about what you see around you as you walk the trails. Three trails are described and pictured; the Sea Lion Point Trail, the Cypress Grove Trail, and the Bird Island Trail.

A one or two-page illustration shows what you see from certain places on the trail, with identifying labels below. Facing the illustration, or following a two-page one, are some words about what you see from where you are standing. Everything changes, and as the years pass over Point Lobos, tree branches fall, bushes grow, birds nest here one spring and there the next, lush gardens after a rainy winter are sparse and dusty after drought, so that what you see from the trail will never be exactly like the picture in the book.

I copied this format from an old Chinese Buddhist pilgrim's guidebook to Mt. Omei, a high mountain in western Szechwan, said to be the abode of the Bodhi-sattva Samantabhadra and a Buddhist shrine for three thousand years. Sixty-four woodblock prints represent views of the path up the mountain, and picture the monasteries, terraces, halls, peaks, stones, bridges, streams, precipices, caverns, plants, beasts, reptiles, weather and historical remnants to which the pilgrims pay homage. Words about the scenes follow the pictures, and forty-six poems celebrate Mt. Omei. The original book was published in 1887 by Huang Shou-fu. It was reprinted in China in 1936 with an English translation by Dryden Phelps, a professor of English literature at West China University; he later lived near Henry Miller on Partington Ridge in Big Sur, California. The drawings were done by T'an Chung-yo, who wandered six months upon the mountain, "taking my brush in its bag.... combing my hair with the wind and washing my head with the rain."* I was so enchanted by this book that I wanted to draw and write one like it, describing some trail I had walked on. The trails of Point Lobos were the right size to put into a book and a trail guide would be useful to the visitors walking there. So, taking my brush in hand and standing on the windy rocks, I made this book.

As I walk around Point Lobos I like to acknowledge the water, rocks, winds, fogs, trees, plants, birds, beasts and creeping beings who together give to me the beauty of this place, and also the people who have come here before me, who, by their care in passing through, have left the beauty unspoiled for me to enjoy.

Frances Thompson

Big Sur, California
May, 1980

*Huang Shou-fu and T'an Chung-yo, trans. Dryden Phelps, Omei Illustrated Guide Book (Hong Kong University Press Reprint as Mount Omei Illustrated Guide, 1974), p. LXXVII.

Point Lobos from the north

ABOUT POINT LOBOS

POINT LOBOS STATE RESERVE
ROUTE 1, BOX 62
CARMEL, CALIFORNIA 93923
TELEPHONE 408/624-4909

LOCATION — Point Lobos is located on State Highway 1, 130 miles south of San Francisco; 345 miles north of Los Angeles; and 4 miles south of Carmel, California.

HOURS — The Reserve is open every day of the year. The hours are posted on the entrance gate. They vary with the season.

GUIDED TOURS — There are guided tours during the summer, and occasionally during other seasons. You can tour the Cypress Grove, Pine Woods, Bird Island, North Shore, Whaler's Cove or Sea Lion Point Trails. There is a tidepool walk held early mornings in summer when weather and tide permit. Inquire at the entrance kiosk.

WAVES — They are more powerful than you expect and can overtake you. Stay a safe distance from the breakers, especially when standing on the rocks.

POISON OAK — Stay on the trails, because contact with leaves or stems can cause swelling, blisters and itching. Leaves grow in groups of three.

THESE LAWS ARE ENFORCED

PARKING — Park only in designated areas.

TRAILS — To avoid damage to the landscape, remain on trails shown on the map. Permitted exceptions are the shorelines at Sea Lion Point, and between Sand Hill Cove and Pebbly Beach.

FIRES AND SMOKING — Stoves and fires of all types are prohibited within the Reserve. Smoking is prohibited on all trails.

PETS — Pets are not permitted on trails or beaches. Leashed pets are allowed only on roadways, parking and picnic areas.

PICNICKING — Picnic only in areas with tables.

COLLECTING — Do not collect, remove or even disturb any natural object in the Reserve, including flowers, wood, rocks and tidepool life.

MARINE RESERVE — Because the adjoining underwater areas are reserves, all fishing is prohibited, and collecting marine life or natural objects is illegal. Diving access only at Whaler's Cove parking lot, with diving permitted in Whaler's and Bluefish Coves.

CLOSURE — Visitors must vacate the Reserve by the closing hour posted at the entrance. Because of the Reserve's small size, the gates close temporarily to the public after 450 people have entered.

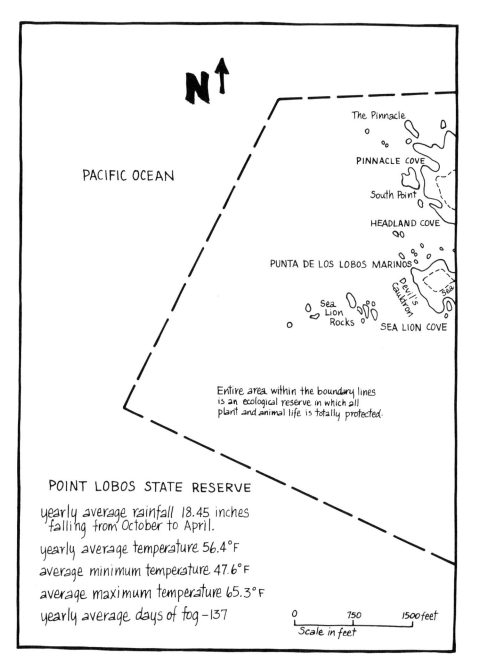

N↑

PACIFIC OCEAN

The Pinnacle

PINNACLE COVE

South Point

HEADLAND COVE

PUNTA DE LOS LOBOS MARINOS

Devil's Cauldron

Sea

Sea
Lion
Rocks

SEA LION COVE

Entire area within the boundary lines
is an ecological reserve in which all
plant and animal life is totally protected.

POINT LOBOS STATE RESERVE

yearly average rainfall 18.45 inches
falling from October to April.

yearly average temperature 56.4°F

average minimum temperature 47.6°F

average maximum temperature 65.3°F

yearly average days of fog –137

0   750   1500 feet
Scale in feet

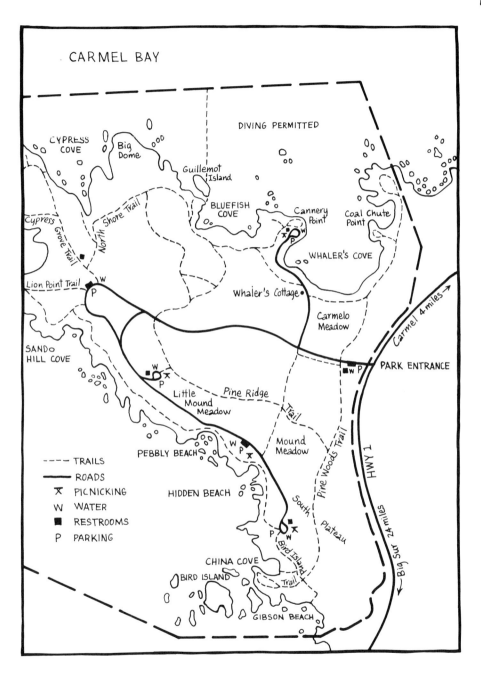

CARMEL BAY

CYPRESS COVE

Big Dome

Guillemot Island

DIVING PERMITTED

North Shore Trail

Cypress Grove Trail

BLUEFISH COVE

Cannery Point

Coal Chute Point

WHALER'S COVE

Lion Point Trail

W
P

Whaler's Cottage

Carmelo Meadow

Carmel 4 miles

SANDo HILL COVE

W
P
X

Little Mound Meadow

Pine Ridge Trail

PARK ENTRANCE

W P

PEBBLY BEACH

W P
X

Mound Meadow

Pine Woods Trail

South Plateau

HWY 1

HIDDEN BEACH

- - - TRAILS
─── ROADS
X PICNICKING
W WATER
■ RESTROOMS
P PARKING

P
W
X

Bird Island

CHINA COVE

BIRD ISLAND

Bird Island Trail

GIBSON BEACH

Big Sur 24 miles

THE SEA LION POINT TRAIL

From the Cypress Grove parking area the **SEA LION POINT TRAIL** takes you across the brushy slope south of Headland Cove to a view of the Sea Lion Rocks, then down among the rocks near the surf. The trail is .6 miles long and it takes about a half an hour to walk down to the ocean and back.

Small birds will be the first of Point Lobos' creatures to greet you on your arrival at the parking area. These **WHITE-CROWNED SPARROWS** are marked with black and white stripes on the head, and under the protection the Reserve extends over all animals within it, they have become quite tame. Home for them is the low bushes of the coastal sage scrub, where they find nesting sites in the branches and pick up seeds and small insects for food, and into which they disappear silently when the shadow or screech of a red-tailed hawk disturbs them.

The resident sub-species of white-crowned sparrow is named <u>nuttalli</u>, after **THOMAS NUTTALL**, an English naturalist who stopped at Monterey in 1836 and may have wandered over Point Lobos collecting plant and animal species. Nuttall was the first experienced scientist to complete a crossing of the North American continent, coming down on the Columbia River from the Rocky Mountains to Fort Vancouver in 1834. On his journeys he was considered a harmless madman, returning delighted from walks across the prairies with collections of what they thought were useless weeds. It was reported that, knowing the guns of the expedition would be kept safe and dry, he used the barrel of his gun as a storage place for packets of seeds.

1 the leaves in threes
Poison Oak
Rhus diversiloba

2 the birds
White-Crowned Sparrows
Zonotrichia leucophrys

1 the jay
  Scrub Jay
  Aphelocoma coerulescens

2 the young tree
  Monterey Cypress
  Cupressus macrocarpa

3 the leaves in threes
  Poison Oak
  Rhus diversiloba

4 the pale aromatic bush
California Sagebrush
Artemisia californica

5 the stiff bush
Coyote Bush
Baccharis pilularis

6 the narrow dark leaves
Northern Sticky Monkeyflower
Mimulus aurantiacus

A young **MONTEREY CYPRESS** grows beside the trail. The seed from which it sprouted was probably carried here by wind or bird or animal; nothing is planted by people at Point Lobos.

On the top branch you might see a **SCRUB JAY.** This is a robin-sized bird, mostly a clear light blue with a buff-colored back, pale under parts, and a dark "necklace" on its throat. It has no crest on its head as does the darker blue Steller's jay. This bird may grab nuts from your picnic, or seeds from the pines and oaks, and bury them in the ground as a reserve food supply. The jay will poke the nut into the earth and pound it deeper with some blows of its long, strong bill. A few flips of the bill and the earth and leaves are scattered over the spot so that you can scarcely find it afterwards, even if you watched the performance. Even the jay sometimes forgets the spot, and thus helps to plant new trees. Jays are conspicuous birds. They perch and flap on the topmost branches of their coastal scrub habitat, screeching at whatever appears to them as a dangerous trespasser through their nesting territory.

One of the common plants all over Point Lobos Reserve is **POISON OAK.** Woe to those who leave the marked trails to plunge into the bushes. On skin contact with its leaves and stems most people develop a mild to severe itchy red rash. The leaves grow in groups of three and resemble oak leaves in form. Poison oak is one of the few plants in the area to turn a pretty rosy or rusty red in the fall; the stems are bare in winter and in spring the new growth is reddish, then shiny bright green, so it is an attractive native species, and itch-producing at all times of year. It is a rampant ground cover, an erosion preventer, a hiding place for birds and other small animals; but for its ability alone to defend off-trail territory from invasion by people, poison oak could be called the guardian deity of Point Lobos.

Point Lobos is a **STATE RESERVE**, and different from a State Park. Reserves are created to preserve a native ecological association, in this case one of the two last remaining native stands of Monterey Cypress in the world plus attendant plants and animals, in an undisturbed condition. Improvements are for the purpose of making the Reserve available for day use by people for their enjoyment and education. Building of some roads, trails and toilets are all the changes people have made here. **STATE PARKS** are scenic areas which allow recreation and may permit camping.

Point Lobos Reserve covers 404 acres; 300,000 people per year visit it. To preserve it in an undisturbed condition, walking and picnicking must be done in designated areas. Anyone walking just a little off the trail to take a photograph or to peer down over a cliff at the ocean is liable to trample new sprouts of cypress trees and to destroy other vegetation, resulting in erosion of the earth beneath.

1. the orange flowers
   Northern Sticky Monkeyflower
   Mimulus aurantiacus

2. the leaves in threes
   Poison Oak
   Rhus diversiloba

3. the male Coyote Bush
   Mr. Fuzzy-Wuzzy
   autumn aspect

4. the female Coyote Bush
   Mrs. Fuzzy-Wuzzy
   autumn aspect

5 the stiff bush
Coyote Bush
  Baccharis pilularis

6 the very narrow leaves
California Sagebrush
  Artemisia californica

7 the scarlet "flower"
Seaside Painted Cup
  Castilleja latifolia

8 the hummingbird
Anna's Hummingbird
  Calypte anna

If you look closely at some of the plants around you along the trail, you'll find these species, and perhaps a humming bird visiting them.

CALIFORNIA SAGEBRUSH is the feathery light greenish-gray aromatic plant growing near the sea all along the California coast from Marin county south. It is not a true sage; it is an <u>Artemisia</u> related to wormwood, a plant of which the liqueur absinthe is made. The sage that cowboys ride through is also an <u>Artemisia</u>. True sages belong to the mint family, have square stems and rough-textured leaves which are strongly aromatic. Hedge Nettle growing at Point Lobos is a true sage, and so is the sage used in cooking, which comes from the Mediterranean region.

Some plant species bear male flowers on one plant and female flowers on another. One of these is **COYOTE BUSH**, one of the most common plants in the coastal sage scrub all over the Reserve. Coyote bush is shown in the picture as it looks most of the year, and also as it appears in late summer, when it is known as Mr. and Mrs. Fuzzy-Wuzzy.

Most of the year you will see **SEASIDE PAINTED CUPS** blooming a vivid scarlet or yellow. The true flower is small; most of the color is on the bracts surrounding each flower. It is a species of paintbrush.

Zooming above your head toward the red paintbrush flowers may be **ANNA'S HUMMINGBIRD**, a permanent resident of Point Lobos. Females are iridescent green with light underparts; males are green also with a flashing, shimmering rosy-red forehead and throat, which looks black until the light hits it just right. Hovering before a flower, the bird pumps nectar through its long tubular tongue. Hummingbirds are the only birds who can fly backwards, and one of the few birds who can hover in one spot in mid-air. They feed on nectar from flowers; a bird consumes half its weight of nectar daily, plus a few small insects.

Hummingbirds must feed constantly during the day to fuel their high metabolism which maintains their body temperature. In order to survive the night without eating, they lower their metabolism and body temperature and drop into a state of torpor akin to the hibernation of mammals.

The Miwok Indians of the Sierra foothills told a story of how this hummingbird was sent by Coyote Man, the creator, to steal fire from the Star Women for the newly created people to cook with. Hummingbird darted into the Star Women's campfire and stole a spark; holding it tight under its chin it brought the fire back to Coyote Man. You can still see the mark of the fire under the hummingbird's chin.

In summer you may also see **ALLEN'S HUMMING-BIRD** with a green back, rufous sides and a fiery orange throat. The birds fly up from Northern Mexico to spend the summer on the California coast.

Looking over Headland Cove to the foot of the granite cliffs, along the water's edge for a hundred yards or so from the beach, you might see a few **HARBOR SEALS** hauled out on the rocks. They are various shades of gray, silver, brown and black, often with spots, and they look a bit like fat sausages with eyes. Indeed they are not as fully articulated as the sea lions. They belong to the family of true seals; they do not have a projecting ear flap nor can they turn their rear flippers underneath themselves and move over the rocks as sea lions can. Out of the water Harbor seals flump along awkwardly. The seals you see loafing in the sun on the rocks swam onto their perches while the tide was high and rested there as the water receded. They are often seen observing their observer from the water, poking out a round face, curious nose and large dark eyes. Scuba divers are sometimes startled to see those dark eyes peering right into their face masks underwater. Like the sea lions, they feed on fish, squid and octopus. They are year around residents and raise their pups on the rocks and cliffs.

Below the seals, at the water line, or on the surf-swept rocks of the headlands at a low tide, you'll see an alga looking like a tiny palm tree and called **SEA PALM.** These "palms" cling to the rocks with tenacious holdfasts and survive the surge of the surf by their flexible nature, giving with the wash of each wave and offering little resistance.

1 the seal
Harbor seal
Foca vitulina

2 the seaweed
Sea Palm
Postelsia palmaeformis

1 the gull
Western Gull
Larus occidentalis

2 the bumpy rock
Carmelo formation

3 the succulent
Sea Fig
Mesembryanthemum chilense

4 the granite cliff
  Santa Lucia Granodiorite

5 the dark trees
  Monterey Cypress
  Cupressus _macrocarpa_

The bumpy, pebbly rock you come toward now is the **CARMELO FORMATION**, a series of conglomerates intermixed with sand and sandy shale. The Carmelo formation is of Paleocene age, 50-60 million years old. It was deposited during a time of sinking coastline, when sediments from the land accumulated near the seashore. Now, when the coast is rising, material eroded from the land is carried out to sea and deposited on the continental shelf. You can see examples of wind erosion on these rocks. Bits of sand carried in Pacific gales hollowed out the peculiar caves and nooks in the seaward side of the hill.

Across Headland Cove you can see the cliffs composed of **SANTA LUCIA GRANODIORITE**, a granite rock that is of early Cretaceous origin, 110 million years old. The core of the northern part of the Santa Lucia Mountains, which drop into the sea along the Big Sur coast south of Point Lobos, is of this rock. From this viewpoint it is clearly seen that the granodiorite is a more resistant rock than the Carmelo sedimentary formation, as Cypress Headland juts boldly out to sea in high cliffs, while the hill you are on is literally being blown away.

A few **WESTERN GULLS** may be standing on top of the rocks, flying high above or swooping below you near the water. They have a dark gray mantle and wings, black wing-tips, a yellow bill, and flesh colored legs. The western gull is the most common gull at Point Lobos, and the only gull that breeds here. You can often see the baby birds on the rocks just off shore.

Plants originating and growing in a region through the ages are called **NATIVE PLANTS.** Plants brought in from other continents or far-away geographical areas are called non-native, exotic or **INTRODUCED PLANTS.** Plants can be introduced by people, sometimes deliberately, sometimes by accident, such as a seed stuck on a shoe or in a pocket. Animals can transport seeds on their fur, birds on their feet and bills or in their gut, and seeds can be blown by the wind or carried by water. A program begun in the summer of 1979 calls for the removal of most non-native species of plants from Point Lobos Reserve. Some of the introduced species are aggressive and crowd out the original native vegetation. Once the exotic plant is removed, the native seeds lying naturally in the soil have space to germinate and grow. Some species are not possible to remove, such as the grass called wild oat, introduced by the Spanish and now growing all over the state. Other species in process of being removed from the Reserve are poison hemlock, broom, periwinkle, oxalis and the very invasive kikuyu grass from Africa. The purpose of a Reserve is to preserve a native ecological association in an undisturbed condition. That makes for a problem in management. Does "undisturbed condition" mean to allow non-native plants "naturally" to invade, or does "preserve a native ecological association" mean to remove the non-native plants? Right now the second choice is being followed.

The succulent growing rampantly north of the trail near the rocks is **SEA FIG** and botanists cannot agree whether it is a native plant or one introduced from South America. This, plus its tenacity as a ground cover, allows it to remain.

 1 the barking animals
Sea Lions

2 the black birds
Cormorants

3 the squirrel
Beechey Ground Squirrel
Spermophilus beecheyi

4 the bumpy rock
Carmelo formation

Suddenly all of the **PUNTA DE LOS LOBOS MARINOS** is before you. Along with the roar of the waves and the sound of the wind in your ears, you can usually hear the sea lions barking from the offshore rocks.

You are sure to be greeted at this spot by the **BEECHEY GROUND SQUIRREL**, begging for handouts. It's best not to feed wild animals; they can find what they need on the earth and then they are not dependent on humans. Besides, they bite. All California rodents could possibly carry the flea which carries the bacillus which causes bubonic plague. Even dead rodents should not be handled. (Plague has not been reported along the coast of Monterey County.) Ground squirrels live colonially in burrows. On the coast where winter temperatures are mild, they do not hibernate, although on a chilly winter day you won't see many of them. They eat seeds, plants and insects, and can be a pest in agricultural fields. Hawks, owls, eagles, rattlesnakes, bobcats, foxes and coyotes control their numbers.

The species name of the ground squirrel, <u>beecheyi</u>, honors **FREDERICK WILLIAM BEECHEY**, commander of the English ship "Blossom", which visited San Francisco and Monterey in 1826. Beechey and his party surveyed San Francisco Bay and made scientific observations and collections. The resulting publication was praised by the historian Bancroft for being more accurate than any preceding navigator. In his great work, the <u>History of California</u>, Bancroft says of Beechey, "had the visitor been less careful and made more blunders, he would receive more attention from me. Such is fame, and the reward of painstaking."

The ocean spread out before you is only the top of the **ECOLOGICAL RESERVE** established in 1973 by the California Department of Fish and Game. All the ocean area surrounding Point Lobos is included in the 750 acres. (see map on pages 14-15). This is the first underwater reserve established in the United States. All marine beings living here are fully protected, so as to create an undisturbed, balanced condition in which all may thrive. No fishing is permitted, no tide pool life or shells may be taken or disturbed. Divers can dive in at Whaler's Cove; diving is permitted in Whaler's Cove and Bluefish Cove. Underneath the surface, divers swim through transparent sunlit water down to the dim bottom, flying among undulating kelp forests, astounded at the waving legs of barnacles, the red plumes of tube worms, the unreal diaphanous iridescent brilliance of nudibranchs (a shell-less mollusc), and all the endless wonders of that exquisite, alien world beneath the sea.

If you look a little north from where you stand, you will be gazing out across ocean water that lies 6,700 feet above the junction of the **CARMEL SUBMARINE CANYON** and the **MONTEREY SUBMARINE CANYON**, 8 miles out to sea. The Grand Canyon full of water would not be as deep. The Carmel Submarine Canyon comes to shore at San Jose Beach, just north of Point Lobos, where the bottom rapidly drops off to several hundred feet. In the spring months deep ocean water rich in mineral nutrients upwells through the canyons to shore, where sunlight allows the growth of plankton to bloom, which supports an unusual diversity of marine life, and helps create the cold water which looks so inviting to swim in, but isn't.

1. the black birds
   Cormorants
   Phalacrocorax sp.

2. the largest sea lion
   male Steller Sea Lion
   Eumetopias jubata

3. the smaller sea lions
   young male California sea lions

4 the large dark sea lion
  male California Sea Lion
  Zalophus californianus
5 the smaller, sleek sea lions
  female California sea lions

6 the red-billed black birds
  Black Oystercatcher
  Haematopus bachmani

Out on the rocks offshore are the Lobos Marinos, the sea wolves, which is what the Spanish called the animal we call the **SEA LION**. When the waves are high and wash over the rocks, the sea lions will be safely out in the open water. Other days you will see them draped gracefully on the rocks engaging in a favorite local pastime of humans and beasts alike, soaking up the brief sunshine. Like many marine mammals (except the sea otter), the sea lions have a thick layer of fat inside their skins to insulate their bodies from the cold ocean water. On the rare days when the sun is truly warm at Point Lobos the sea lions overheat while lying on the rocks. They must go back into the sea to cool themselves during the day. A sea lion is able to turn its hind flippers forward under the body, and thus it can climb rocks and move about on land rather well. Sea lions feed on squid, octopus and fish.

There are two species of sea lions here. The **CALIFORNIA SEA LION** is the smaller, darker brown one, ranging from the islands off the coast of Baja California to Año Nuevo Island north of Santa Cruz, California. The name of the genus, _Zalophus_, comes from the Greek words _zale_, the surging of the sea, and _ophion_, a fabulous animal. The California Sea Lion can live in fresh water and it is the "seal" you see doing tricks in the circus. The males develop a sagittal crest by which you can tell them apart from the females, whose heads are streamlined.

The less common **STELLER SEA LION** is twice as large as the California and has a light buff-colored coat. The bulls average 1,400 lbs. and 10-11 feet in length. The name of the species, <u>jubata</u>, is Latin and means having a mane. The thick mane of the male Steller suggested to people the name sea lion. This northern species ranges from the islands off Southern California north to the Bering Sea. The females are much smaller than the males.

It is a common myth that the male sea lion collects and controls a "harem" of females. Biologists who studied the sea lions on their breeding grounds found that the males arrive first and occupy territories on whichever beaches or rocks are favored by females for a breeding site. The bulls defend the boundaries of their territories by display and fighting. When the females arrive, they wander at will over the beach and move without restraint through the various territories held by the bulls. The bull who mates with the most females is the one who happens to occupy a territory so favored by the females that more of them spend time there. The bulls do not possess female sea lions, they possess space on the beach.

CORMORANTS are the slinky black birds silhouetted against the sea on top of the rocks and flying low over the water.

Looking rather like a crow with a large bright red bill and stout pale legs, the **BLACK OYSTERCATCHER** might be picking over the rocks by the water line. Although not a rare species, it's not commonly encountered throughout its range of the cool Pacific coast from the Aleutians to Baja California. At Point Lobos this bird is easily seen. Its piercing whistle calls your attention to it. The heavy bill is used to pry limpets off rocks, and to break the shells of mussels and barnacles.

1 the dark pines
Monterey Pine
Pinus radiata

2 the bushes
Coastal Sage Scrub

3 the yellow flowers
Lizard Tail Yarrow
Eriophyllum staechadifolium

4 the hawk
Red-Tailed Hawk
Buteo jamaicensis

5 the succulent
Sea fig
Mesembryanthemum chilense

From the top of the hill looking towards the parking area you will see a gray-green sweep of low bushes forming a plant community botanists call the **COASTAL SAGE SCRUB.** Here at Point Lobos the principal plants are California sage, poison oak, coyote bush, lizard tail, mock heather, ceanothus, wild rose, monkey flower and bush lupine, with other herbs and grasses mixed in. Archibald Menzies, a Scots botanist traveling with Vancouver in 1792, who stopped at Monterey and thought the Spanish fandango danced there "would decompose the gravity of a Stoic", took a walk through the scrub and found it "diffused in this dry Country an aromatic fragrance which was exceeding pleasant." In addition to its offering of fragrance, the scrub gives to us pretty flowers throughout most of the year, holds the earth from erosion and provides food and cover for numerous birds and mammals, reptiles and insects. These plants thrive in dry soil and moist sea air, survive salt spray and sprout back green after a fire.

FIRE has been controlled at Point Lobos since it became a Reserve in 1933. Down wood, dead trees and bushes, leaf litter and pine needles have been allowed to rest where they lay, slowly to decompose into new soil. This is the natural state of being of these hills and woods; however, an occasional fire is also natural. Considering the accumulation of dry dead wood in the Reserve, the Park Department has decided on a program of controlled burning to reduce the hazard of a large, uncontrolled and dangerous fire devastating the park. The piles of dead branches are important cover and nest sites for the birds and small mammals, so that it is not easy at all for people to maintain the same balance that nature does — among cover for animals, too much dead wood, and fire.

Most of the plants and trees of this coastal plant community are well adapted to an occasional fire since fires have been in their lives throughout the ages of their evolution. The scrub bushes spring up new shoots from their root crowns immediately after the first rain following a fire. Some wild flowers, such as lupine, produce seeds which sprout more readily after a fire has passed over them and burnt off their hard seed coat. The **MONTEREY PINE**, whose shadowy crowns accent the pale scrub, has cones which persist on the branches for years and remain closed until a particularly hot day or a fire causes them to open and scatter their seeds, beginning a new, post-fire generation. The several species of these **CLOSED-CONE PINES** all grow in brushy, dry summer areas where fires have always been frequent.

Soaring high in the air may be a **RED-TAILED HAWK.** When it swoops down after a ground squirrel, you can see the chestnut-red of the upper surface of the tail. This hawk is common in most habitats all over the west. Hawks catch and eat small mammals, birds and reptiles. Their hunting is important in keeping rodent populations under control.

1 the stalk of flowers
Bush Lupine
<u>Lupinus</u> <u>arboreus</u>

2 the seed pod
Lupine seeds

3 the butterfly
Monarch Butterfly
<u>Danaus</u> <u>plexippus</u>

4 the yellow flowers
  Lizard-Tail Yarrow
    Eriophyllum staechaditolium

5 the bird
  Wren-Tit
    Chamaea fasciata

6 the stickery plant
  Mock Heather
    Haplopappus ericoides

Here are some of the plants you will see in the coastal scrub, and a bird you might hear.

The large spikes of yellow or lavender-blue sweet-pea-like flowers are **BUSH LUPINE**, and are indeed a pea. The name lupine comes from the Latin _lupus_, a wolf, and refers to an ancient notion that lupines rob the soil of nutrients. How this notion got about is a mystery, since all peas, clovers, beans and other legumes have nodules on their roots which contain bacteria that fix nitrogen in the soil. Legumes are often grown as cover crops to improve soil. This bush lupine is an important plant to the birds of Point Lobos. It produces abundant large seeds the birds like to eat. Its bushy growth provides nesting places attractive to the white-crowned sparrow. Underneath the lupine, dead leaves and other litter collects, creating habitat for insects and food foraging for the California Thrasher, the Rufous-sided Towhee, and other birds and small mammals. The exposed top branches are used as look-out perches by California Thrashers, Black Phoebes, Western Bluebirds and Shrikes.

LIZARD-TAIL YARROW is another common Point Lobos plant, with a handsomely designed linear leaf which reminded someone of a lizard tail, and bright yellow flowers in spring and summer.

MOCK HEATHER is the stickery plant with needle-like leaves growing alongside the lizard tail and bush lupine. It blooms later in the year than other Point Lobos flowers, beginning to blossom its yellow flowers in late August. The name of the genus is _Haplopappus_, from the Greek _haplos_, meaning simple or single, and the Latin _pappus_, or plant down, from the Greek _pappos_, the first down on the cheek, all of which is to say the mature seeds are fuzzy. The downy fuzz is attached to the seed; wind blows both to a new growing site.

Heard but not often seen will be the **WREN-TIT**, a brown, sparrow-sized bird with a long cocked tail, a lightly streaked breast and a pale eye. This common California bird usually flits among the bushes, rarely showing itself. The bird's ringing call, once compared to a Model T Ford starting up -----rr----rr---rr--rr-rrrr- always accompanies a walk through the coastal scrub.

On fine sunny days from October through March you will see the **MONARCH BUTTERFLY** flying brilliantly red-orange against the clear blue winter sky. Below 55° the butterflies cannot fly, so on cool days they cluster together on tree branches with wings overlapping, which gives them warmth, and protection from being blown away by the wind. At Point Lobos different trees are used each year as resting places by the butterflies. In spring the Monarchs fly towards Northern California, Oregon and perhaps as far as Canada. They mate and lay eggs along the way. The caterpillars eat milkweeds and transform into new Monarchs. Their life span is about 9 months, so those butterflies who head south to escape the northern winter are not the ones who flew north in spring.

THE CYPRESS GROVE TRAIL

1. the coarse grass
Giant Wild Rye
Elymus condensatus

2. the pale aromatic bush
California Sagebrush
Artemisia californica

3. the leaves in threes
Poison Oak
Rhus diversiloba

4. the rabbit
Brush Rabbit
Sylvilagus bachmani

5 the largest bush
Wild Lilac
Ceanothus thyrsiflorus

6 the pale green shreds
Lace Lichen
Ramalina reticulata

7 the orange flowers
Northern Sticky Monkeyflower
Mimulus aurantiacus

8 the soft furry leaves
Wood Mint
Stachys bullata

The **CYPRESS GROVE TRAIL** begins at the northwest end of the Cypress Cove parking area. It is a loop of 0.7 miles and takes about three-quarters of an hour to walk around. The trail takes you through a cypress grove growing above high granite cliffs; between the trees you see spectacular vistas of rocks, waves and water, glimpses of the Monterey Peninsula and a wide view of the open Pacific. The first picture is seen about a hundred feet down the trail from the trail sign.

If you walk this path in early spring, February to April, the exuberant sprays of bright blue **WILD LILAC**, or ceanothus, will enchant your eyes. There are almost a hundred species and sub-species of this common scrub plant in California, plus some hybrids created for garden and freeway ornament. Four species are found at Point Lobos. Like many plants of the dry hillsides, wild lilac is evergreen and has small, hard-coated leaves which resist dehydration. The flowers are fragrant.

Below the lilac bushes are mint-like plants with small purple flowers in spring, called **HEDGE NETTLE** or **WOOD MINT**. The plant belongs to the mint family, as you can tell by examining a stem; it is square, not round.

The large grass spears rising above the bushes on the south side of the path are **GIANT WILD RYE**. This is a native grass which grows sparsely but commonly amongst the chaparral and coastal sage scrub in Central and Southern California. The Indians are said to have gathered the seeds for food.

Gray-green cobwebby shreds of **LACE LICHEN** add a gloomy touch to bare branches of ceanothus, and from the dead wood in the dark shade under the cypresses they waver in the foggy wind. Black-tailed deer rear up to eat all the lichen they can reach. Birds use it to line their nests and keep their babies cozy, and so did the Ohlone Indians, who made diapers out of it.

LICHENS aren't parasites; they did not kill the branches they grow on here, which probably died of wind exposure and salt spray. Lichens are composed of two plants that act as helpful partners to each other in a relationship called mutualism. One plant is a fungus; mushrooms are a common fungus. The other plant is an alga; seaweeds are algae. The fungus collects water and provides a tough frame-work and a protective coat for the algal cells embedded within it. Fungi lack chlorophyll and therefore can't manufacture their own food. The algae contain chlorophyll and produce sugar for themselves and the fungus, using water and nutrients supplied by the fungus plus energy from the sun in a process called photosynthesis. So this dead-looking stuff hanging from the trees is actually dancing with marvelous co-operative activity.

Hopping across the trail in front of you may be a **BRUSH RABBIT,** a common resident of the Reserve.

Take the right hand trail at the junction marked with the sign "A. M. Allen Memorial Grove".

1 the dark tree
Monterey Cypress
Cupressus macrocarpa

2 the grass
Wild Oat
Avena fatua

3 the white flowers
Yarrow
Achillea borealis

4 under the sea
  Carmel Submarine Canyon

5 the white sand
  Carmel Beach

6 the bush
  Ceanothus sp.

Growing in this sunny patch of meadow is **WILD OAT.**
Brilliant green in winter and spring, wild oat dries out to
a bleached gold as the rains stop, becoming California's
famous golden hills and partially accounting for the name
Golden State. Although the grass grows everywhere in
California, it is not a native species, having been introduced
by the Spaniards about 1800 when the missions were built
along the coast. Botanists made studies of seeds found in
adobe bricks from old buildings whose construction dates
were known and discovered that in the earliest buildings,
constructed before 1769, the date of the establishment of
the first mission, no wild oat seed was to be found. After
1800, wild oat seed was abundant in adobe bricks from
the San Francisco Bay region and after 1857 an observer
reported that wild oat covered many hundreds of miles of
land in central and southern California. The native
grasses were perennial bunch grasses and perennial clovers.
These disappeared with the overstocking of cattle on the
range lands. There are some other species of grass in the
meadow, but only wild oat has the characteristic panicle
drawn in the picture.

The head of many tiny white flowers with feathery dark
green aromatic foliage is **YARROW.** Each tiny flower is
like a miniature daisy, so the plant belongs to the family
Compositae. The Indians used the leaves to make a tea for colds.

Across blue Carmel Bay you can see a brilliant white line of
sand against the dark pines of the hills; **CARMEL BEACH.**

Soon after Carmel was first created by real estate developers in 1903, it was a small village among the pines beside the beautiful beach, so charming as to attract many artists, poets, writers and even university professors, who built houses there. The poet George Sterling used to collect his friends, including the writers Jack London, Mary Austin and Upton Sinclair, with the painter Xavier Martinez, and off they would go for a picnic at Point Lobos. Point Lobos was not yet a State Reserve, and people roamed at will to picnic where they pleased and collect abalone off the rocks, being a favorite pastime of the Carmel crowd who wrote a bookfull of verses about the abalone. Even in those days the traffic in Point Lobos was enough to cause erosion of the scarce top soil, and some of the old cypresses people came especially to see were in danger of falling over cliffs into the sea, their roots exposed by the tramping feet of admirers. At last, after Point Lobos became a State Reserve in 1933, the Park Department arranged a system of trails which include the loveliest and most interesting sights, and began to ask people to stay on those trails. 300,000 people a year visit Point Lobos, and if only one in a hundred goes off the trail "just a few feet so I can get a better shot of that tree there", that's 6,000 shoes per year crushing vegetation, wearing away soil and starting the erosion of a ragged gully.

Between you and Carmel lies very deep water. The upper end of the **CARMEL SUBMARINE CANYON** runs up toward the shore just north of Point Lobos. The water you are looking across is about 1200 feet deep.

1 the trees
Monterey Cypress
Cupressus _macrocarpa_

2 the pale green shreds
Lace Lichen
Ramalina reticulata

3 the birds
Dark-Eyed Junco
  Junco _hyemalis_

Now the trail enters one of the last native stands of Monterey Cypress left on earth. Its being here today undesecrated for us to behold is due to the intention of **MR. A. M. ALLEN**, for whom the grove is named; he was the person who made it his responsibility to preserve Point Lobos as it is, rather than have it divided up into straight right-angle streets of twenty-five foot lots and called Pt. Lobos City, as was planned at the time Allen began to acquire property there in 1898.   At that time Point Lobos was owned by the Carmelo Land and Coal Co., which had been mining coal in the mountains south-east of Point Lobos and loading it on board ships at Coal Shute Point. Mr. Allen had knowledge of coal mining, and bought a large tract of the coal company's land. By this time the coal operation had closed down, and a resort sub-division was laid out on paper straight across a piece of Point Lobos' lovely hills and woods. Allen built a ranch house, in which he lived thirty-two years until his death, and he began to buy back the lots sold to prospective residents of Pt. Lobos City, or Carmelito. He stated his intention as, "It is my hope to preserve this property in its natural state for the enjoyment of those who appreciate nature, provided that such use will not get beyond control and become a menace to the property itself." When Point Lobos became a State Reserve in 1933, this grove was given as a gift to the people from the Allen family and it is dedicated as a memorial to A.M. Allen and his wife, Satie Morgan Allen.

The **MONTEREY CYPRESS** has one of the most restricted distributions of any coniferous species in the world. Only one other native grove exists, across Carmel Bay at Cypress Point. All Monterey Cypress you ever see away from

Cypress Point or Point Lobos have been planted by people, or are descended from trees that were. The tree is easily grown from seed and becomes a large handsome tree in suitable climates around the world, so we wonder why its native range is so small.

Perhaps in the Pleistocene epoch when the climate was cooler and wetter than it is now, large forests of cypress grew along the coast. When the climate warmed up and became drier, the cypress population shrank into areas that remained cool and damp, so botanists suspect. Only with the help of people can the tree cross the hot, dry regions of California to become established in other, cooler areas.

At Point Lobos new trees sprout and grow here and there. As far as observers can tell, this grove of cypresses is slowly extending. The oldest trees are two or three hundred years old.

You may see some **JUNCOS** fluttering over the ground. Juncos are sparrow-sized birds with dull black hoods, easily recognized by the white outer tail feathers that flash as the bird flies. Juncos have thick strong bills adapted for cracking seeds. Their habitat is conifers or mixed forest; they nest on the ground in thickets. The resident junco is known as the Dark-Eyed Junco. It was recently known as the Oregon Junco. Every so often biologists reclassify and rename some plant and animal species, the better to reflect their true relationships. Ideas about true relationships change through the years, so one must buy a new book now and then to stay up on the fashion, although the birds in the trees look pretty much the same year after year.

1 the pines
  Monterey Pine
    Pinus *radiata*

2 the granite
  Santa Lucia Granodiorite

3 the seaweed
  Kelp

4 the dark tree
Monterey cypress
Cupressus macrocarpa

5 the violet-blue flowers
Douglas Iris
Iris douglasiana

This view is reached by turning right at the first junction you come to. The side trail is very short.

From this perch you can look down to the blue ocean sliding off the granite rocks, and across to cypresses and pines growing on the cliffs. The **GRANODIORITE ROCK** has been lifted above the sea and into the wind for less than half a million years, just a wink of geologic time.

In March and April the **DOUGLAS IRIS** will be blooming violet-blue flowers; at other times of year you will see the graceful grasslike blades of the leaves. Iris means rainbow in Greek and Douglas is David Douglas, a Scotsman sent out by the Horticultural Society of London to collect plants in the 1820's and 30's. Imagine spacemen returning from a far planet with marvelous new flowers never seen before, and you will understand why, after the first voyages of exploration returned from the New World with their botanical treasures, plant dealers hired people to travel the world collecting specimens and seeds of the new plants. Douglas introduced more plants into cultivation than any other collector of his time, and discovered many new ones, such as the huge fir named after him. He was a fair-skinned, crabby tempered man, by all accounts, who was in Monterey in 1831. He thought the California sun abominable, complained that the heat was "so intense as to suffocate the fleas", and seemed to prefer sleeping out in the rain of the Columbia River country, where he spent much time collecting. While walking in the Hawaiian Islands with his pack, collecting kit and ever-present little dog, he fell into a pit-trap containing a wild bull and was trampled to death.

You might see a **SEA OTTER** swimming in the cove, or floating on its back in the kelp beds. Look carefully, it's easy to mistake the round floats of the kelp for a mammal head. **KELP** is the brown seaweed floating just under the surface of the water.

As you walk from this cove on through Cypress Grove you will see bits of bright sea shells in the soil underfoot. These are remains of **INDIAN SHELLMOUNDS**. A tribe of Ohlone Indians called the Rumsen and their ancestors as far back as 2,000 years, as dated by charcoal from the village of Ichxenta located across the highway from Point Lobos Reserve, wandered here foraging for abalone, mussels, fish and other seashore food. They must have shucked their catches here and there on Point Lobos and left the shells behind in piles. There was no permanent village on Point Lobos as there is no permanent spring or creek of fresh water in the Reserve.

1️⃣ the succulent rosettes
Bluff Lettuce
Dudleya farinosa

2️⃣ the trees
Monterey Cypress
Cupressus macrocarpa

3️⃣ the lavender daisy
Seaside Daisy
Erigeron glaucus

4 the red fuzz
Algae
Trentepohlia aurea

5 the rock
Pinnacle Rock

Next on the trail is another short side-trail to the right that leads to a spectacular view of the Monterey Peninsula across Carmel Bay. The main trail passes under dark cypress branches through which you glimpse bright flashes of sun-lit surf and silver granite, or, on a summer day, a quiet gray sea and a white gull flying, its lone cry softened by thick fog. This view shows **PINNACLE COVE**, and the jutting granite rock called **PINNACLE ROCK**.

Even if it is calm and quiet as you walk here, you can tell by looking at the trees that this rocky point receives the ocean winds directly off the open Pacific. In response to the strain of the wind blowing on the crown of the tree, the branches and trunk develop **BUTTRESSING**, with the narrow edge of the trunk facing the prevailing wind and the depth of the wood behind supporting the trunk. It is also the winds which prune the foliage flat on exposed trees that in sheltered places would grow straight with open, regular crowns. The power of the great invisible winds have carved the famous and fantastic shapes of Point Lobos cypress.

Growing on the trunks and on the lower bare branches of the cypress trees is a **RED FUZZ**. It's **ALGAE**, a plant similar to the seaweed in the ocean. The algae are harmless to the trees and manufacture their own food. As the cypress tree grows, its dense canopy of branches shut out the sunlight from the lower foliage, which dies, leaving the scraggly bones to which the algae attach. The red color comes from a plant pigment, carotene, the pigment that makes carrots orange.

Along the trail beneath the trees you will see, in the late spring and summer, a violet-blue daisy with a yellow center called **SEASIDE DAISY**. The plant is a perennial usually found close to the seashore.

If you were a native of the country walking through these woods in 1542, you might have looked between the cypress branches to behold a Spanish sailing ship out to sea. It was Cabrillo, coasting California and bringing back to Mexico news of a new land. He noted a "Cabo de Pinos" (Cape of Pines) but no one knows exactly where it was. After Cabrillo, a few Manila galleons touched California. In 1602, Viscaino made a careful survey of the coast, named Rio del Carmelo, Punta de los Pinos (Point Pinos in Pacific Grove), and Monterey Bay. Viscaino and his men camped in freezing, wet weather just north of Point Lobos. The Spanish always referred to these sea lion covered rocks as **PUNTA DE LOS LOBOS MARINOS**, or Point of the Sea Wolves, and after all "wolves" isn't any sillier than "lions" for those large slippery animals which are related to bears. When the Anglos came to Monterey, they called the place Point Lobos.

Growing on the shaded granite rock to the left of the stone steps are gray-green succulent rosettes dusted with sticky gray powder. They are a native seaside plant called **BLUFF LETTUCE**. At the end of summer the plants bear long stems of yellow flowers. They are also called Stonecrop, and belong to the Liveforever genus, both apt names. New plants sprout off the old ones so that each group of rosettes is actually the same plant and hundreds of years old.

1 the whales
California Gray Whale
Eschrichtius robustus

2 the granite
Santa Lucia Granodiorite

3 the gulls
  Western Gull
  Larus occidentalis

4 the point
  Cypress Point

5 the succulent
  Sea Fig
  Mesembryanthemum chilense

Walking up the stone steps and around the bend you come to **SOUTH POINT** where you can walk out on the very edge of the granite cliffs. Winter storms can blow up immense waves against these rocks. One terrific storm in 1960 washed out a section of the trail where you stand.

During late December and in January the **CALIFORNIA GREY WHALE** may come close to the rocks of Point Lobos on its migration from the Bering Sea to Baja California. This 12,000 mile round trip is made each year by the whales, who leave their summer feeding grounds off the coasts of Alaska and Siberia in autumn and begin to move south along the North American coast, averaging about two hundred miles per day until in early spring they arrive at the warm lagoons in Baja California, where the females give birth. Some mothers with calves may remain in the lagoons as late as May, while the other whales have already left for the cold, plankton-rich Arctic waters.

Watch the surface of the ocean during late December and January and you may see a spray of white water vapor in the air—a whale spouting at the surface! With binoculars you can see its mottled gray skin; some of the white spots are barnacles. Grey whales have baleen, a series of fringed plates suspended from the roof of their mouths, with which they strain out of the ocean water the tons of tiny crustaceans and other plankton creatures they eat, building up blubber for the long yearly journey.

There was a picturesque **PORTUGUESE WHALING STA-TION** in Whaler's Cove at Point Lobos from the 1860's through 1884. Whales were harpooned from small boats put out from shore, towed back, and the blubber stripped and boiled to extract the oil. Neat white houses and gardens surrounded the cove, and from Carmel mission people could hear the grizzly bears growling over the remains of the whales washed up on the beaches north of Point Lobos. The whales were almost exterminated; now they are protected. Their encouraging increase in numbers shows people that what they do can make a difference for the wonderful lives of the animals around us on the earth. The Humpback Whale, the Sei Whale and the flashy black and white Killer all visit Point Lobos occasionally.

Down below you, creeping among the rocks hidden under water are **ABALONES.** Abalones like rocky shores; they hide in dark cracks between rocks and come out to graze upon kelp and other algae. They are molluscs, belonging, with the common garden snail, to the family of Gastropods, "belly-footed", because their entrails lie under a single shell above a tough, muscular foot. Seven thousand years ago, as dated by old shells from shellmounds, California's native Americans were eating abalone and trading the beautiful shell along trade routes reaching as far as Colorado.

White folks wouldn't eat abalone when they arrived in California, but the Chinese did, and soon had a busy fishery, canning abalone to sell to China. The Japanese divers with diving suits began going deeper to find more and larger abalone than the depleted shoreline offered, and by the 1890's an abalone cannery was established at Point Lobos near Whaler's Cove. The buildings have since been demolished.

1 the seaweed
Kelp

2 the grass
Wild Oat
Avena fatua

3 the tree
Monterey Cypress
Cupressus macrocarpa

4 the pale aromatic plant
California Sagebrush
Artemisia californica

5 the silver-green leaves
Bush Lupine
Lupinus arboreus

The trail continues around on the south, sunny side of the point, through a cypress woods with views of the Sea Lion Rocks across Headland Cove. On a summer day you may not be able to see the Rocks, and only the barks of the sea lions will sound softly through the blowing fog. You had hoped for a sunny picnic and now you are freezing in a cold wind. Why is it so gloomy here in summer?

Several factors create the condition of **SUMMER FOG** on the coast of Central California. The heart of the system is a permanent area of high air pressure over the eastern North Pacific Ocean. This high pressure area is southerly and weak in winter. In summer it moves north and becomes stronger. The edge of the clockwise circle of wind forming the high pressure area touches the coastline in summer, becoming the prevailing wind blowing from the north-west. Due to physical laws of the universe, when a wind blows parallel to a coast with the coast on its left, ocean currents are deflected towards the right. Thus surface water is carried away from shore, and cold deep water flows upward to replace it, resulting in cold summer sea water near the shore. Also, the air above this cold water cools, creating a temperature inversion with dry interior air aloft. This warm air from the interior, the normal California summer condition, cannot mix with the cool ocean air due to the coast ranges being in the way, dropping straight into the sea with almost no coastal plain. The cool air over the ocean condenses around salt particles, forming fog.

Most of the brown seaweed in the water of Cypress Cove is **KELP**. Kelps are large brown algae, simple plants that reproduce without flowers or seeds. They attach to the bottom of the cove by a tangle of root-like strands called a holdfast. Kelp forests provide habitats for innumerable marine creatures; from tiny bryozoa living on the brown fronds, to crabs, snails, various rockfish and perch, abalone, the sea urchin and its predator, the sea otter. In Southern California, where sea otters are extinct, sea urchins began to wipe out the vast kelp beds offshore by eating the lower parts of the plants. When the urchins were controlled by people, the kelp returned luxuriantly. Here in the Monterey Bay area, our sea otters dine on enough sea urchins to keep the natural balance intact; our kelp forests flourish and so do the creatures living among them. In addition to sheltering beautiful and useful marine life, kelp yields a chemical called algin, which gives tall seaweeds the resilience to withstand life in the surging waves. Kelp is harvested with huge barges that mow a twenty foot swath through the beds, and the algin is extracted, to be used as a stabilizer and thickener. It's a common additive in ice cream and many other products. Kelp has long been used for food in Oriental countries. Kelp and other ocean algae are one of the few non-meat sources of the essential vitamin B_{12}. As meat becomes increasingly expensive and inefficient to produce, kelp might be an important food for the whole world in the future.

THE BIRD ISLAND TRAIL

1 the squirrel
Western Gray Squirrel
 Sciurus griseus

2 the upside-down bird
Pygmy Nuthatch
 Sitta pygmaea

3 the pine
Monterey Pine
Pinus radiata

4 the blue bird
Steller's Jay
Cyanocitta stelleri

You can walk to the Bird Island parking area from the entrance gate by following the Pine Woods trail, or drive there, following the main road along the southern shore of the Reserve to its end. If you stay for a picnic at the Bird Island picnic tables, you are apt to be visited by these two woods creatures, the **GRAY SQUIRREL** and the **STELLER'S JAY**.

Sciurus griseus is the scientific name of the **GRAY SQUIRREL**. _Sciurus_ is from the Greek _skia_, a shadow or phantom; _griseus_ means gray. Rather bold for a phantom, the squirrel will zip up to inspect you and just as suddenly will vanish up into the pine trees, chugging its loud rubber-duck call. The squirrels make large weatherproof nests of branches, leaves and pine needles high up in the pine trees. Walking along a woods trail in the Reserve you will often find on the ground fallen pine sprays along with scales cut from the cone by the squirrel who demolished it hunting for nuts

Guard your lunch from the large handsome blue jay of the pine woods, the **STELLER'S JAY**, which ranges from the coast of Alaska through the coniferous forests of the west to Central America. For a glimpse of one of nature's outrageous faces, try to get a head-on look at this jay — two vivid beady eyes on either side of a dark head shooting a ragged crest straight up in the air, set off with a few wild stripes of white war paint. The bird's head, shoulders and chest are blackish and the back, wings and tail are an electric cobalt blue. Steller's jays make a confusing variety of squawks, grumbles, squeaks and songs, and when they begin to imitate other birds and finally screech just like a red-tailed hawk, only the most astute bird student can name the singer.

The Steller's jay and the Steller sea lion would have been named Stöler if Georg Wilhelm Stöler hadn't gone from Germany to Russia in 1734, where there was no Russian character to express the sound of his name, and he accepted Steller as the closest approximation. **STELLER** was a naturalist who first discovered and described both those animals and the sea otter. He accompanied Bering on a hazardous journey across Siberia and on by ship into the unknown sea to the east. The expedition was sent out to confirm reports of land to the east of the Pacific.

The water supply ran low as the ships sailed blind through the fog for days in July, 1741. The fog lifted and a shining white mountain rose above dark green spruce. They named it Mount St. Elias as it was that saint's feast day, and this great mountain in southeast Alaska still bears the name. Having accomplished his mission Bering ordered the ships to turn back as soon as water casks were refilled on a small island. After years of terrible hardships Steller had only a few hours to collect specimens of pressed plants and animal skins in the new land. He collected a few plants and a blue jay. During his studies in Germany and Russia Steller had seen colored drawings of Carolina jays. He knew jays were New World birds, so he knew the land he stood on was America. He was the first white man to walk upon Alaska. He collected the sea lion and the sea otter from Alaska shores. The expedition was caught by winter storms on an Aleutian Island where Bering died. Steller died traveling through Siberia with the remains of his collections on his way to the scientific community at St. Petersburg.

1. the pines
Monterey Pine
Pinus radiata

2. the stiff bush
Coyote bush
Baccharis pilularus

3. the white or pink pom-poms
Buckwheat
Eriogonum parvifolium

4. the squirrel
Beechey Ground Squirrel
Spermophilus beecheyi

5 | the coarse grass
Giant Rye Grass
Elymus condensatus

6 | the succulent rosettes
Bluff-Lettuce
Dudleya farinosa

7 | the yellow flowers
Lizard-Tail Yarrow
Eriophyllum staechadifolium

The **BIRD ISLAND TRAIL** rises up the steps south of the south turn parking area, traverses the hillside facing China Cove, winds above Gibson Beach and loops around a jagged promontory with a good view of the birds and animals on Bird Island. The trail is .7 miles long and takes about 20 minutes to walk around.

First the trail enters the edge of the forest shadow cast by the lovely dark **MONTEREY PINES.** This pine is native to several widely separated localities along the Pacific coast. Trees grow north of Santa Cruz, at Monterey, at Cambria Pines and on islands off the coast of Baja California. At Monterey, the trees grow inland six or seven miles, and south down the coast in a narrow strip to Mal Paso Creek, where they stop abruptly. Botanists speculate that the pine, like the cypress, is a relic of a larger distribution in the past, during a time of cool, wet climate. As the climate became warmer and drier, the pine trees died out in most areas and only survived in spots still cool and wet enough to support them. And, like cypress, Monterey pine cannot spread by itself from its native habitat to another congenial spot. The intervening hot, dry areas of California prevent the growth of seedlings. However, aided by admiring humans, the tree has been planted round the world and has a wider horticultural distribution than any other California tree. It is a fast growing and short-lived tree, with a life of perhaps sixty years. It is grown for timber in Australia, Africa, Spain and New Zealand. Because we still have more valuable timber trees in the Douglas fir and the yellow and sugar pines, the Monterey pine has not yet been exploited much in this country.

This is a three needle pine, meaning that there are three needles to a fascicle. If you examine a cluster of **PINE NEEDLES** you will see that three needles are grouped together in a bundle with a brown paper-like wrapping at their base called a fascicle. There are pines with one, two, three, and five needles to a fascicle, and several pines in most categories, so that the number of needles is only one character one must note when identifying a tree. A little wonder of pines is that no matter what the number of needles in a bundle, they will always form a circle when held together – ⊕ and ⊗.

High in the pines you will hear the constant tweet-tweet-tweet of the **PIGMY NUTHATCH**, a small bird with a blue-gray back and white throat and belly that you might see hanging upside-down from a branch, picking insects. They chip out nesting cavities high in the trees, thirty feet or more from the ground.

In July and August the low, round, dry-looking bushes of **WILD BUCKWHEAT** suddenly pop out small pom-poms of white, yellowish or pink flowers in all directions. Bees love the flowers. Buckwheat honey is thick, dark and fragrant.

BEECHEY GROUND SQUIRRELS will beg you for food. Don't feed them, they should not become dependent on hand-outs from people. They naturally eat seeds, plants and insects which are abundant here.

1 the pines
Monterey Pine
Pinus *radiata*

2 a dead pine

3 the succulent rosettes
Bluff Lettuce
Dudleya farinosa

4 the pale aromatic bush
California Sagebrush
Artemisia californica

5 the fringed seaweed
Egregia menziesii

6 the graceful kelp
Giant Kelp
Macrocystis pyrifera

7 the brown floats
Bull Kelp
Nereocystis luetkiana

CHINA COVE *must be one of the prettiest beaches anywhere. If only the water were not so icy cold! Swimming is allowed, if you can bear it, picnicking is not.*

The succulent rosettes you see growing on the rocks on both sides of China Cove are not the same. Those on the north-facing shady cliff beneath the pines are the grayish-green **BLUFF LETTUCE**, and on the south-facing rocks below the trail grows a brighter green **SEA LETTUCE**, reddish at the base of the leaves. There aren't many plants of sea-lettuce close to the trail, but if you examine the rocks below as you walk along, you will see it. Another succulent, sea fig, also grows here. Sea lettuce grows in rosettes, sea fig grows in a dense mat.

Floating in the cove, brown against the transparent turquoise water over the white sand, are various sea-weeds. One has long reddish-brown stipes with a fringe on each side, called _Egregia_. There are two species of kelp, Giant Kelp and Bull Kelp. **GIANT KELP** is a perennial plant, and can grow as much as two feet a day, to become a waving frond 150 feet from its holdfast in the depths to the tip lying along the top of the water. Giant kelp is the most common kelp around Point Lobos and grows in great masses under the summer light. Later in the year, weakened plants are washed up on shore in dry, flyblown tangles by winter storm waves. The frond rises and floats on the water by means of gasfilled bladders along the stipe. Instead of many small bladders, the entire upper third of the **BULL KELP** stipe plus a round float at the end are gasfilled and support the plant. The dark brown, shiny, bobbing floats look much like the heads of seals or sea otters from a distance.

Kelp and most other seaweeds are **ALGAE**, simple plants that reproduce without flowers or seeds. Perhaps 90% of the photosynthesis on earth is accomplished by algae. Photosynthesis is a process during which plants absorb carbon dioxide and release oxygen, using light energy from the sun. Those waving brown strands below you and their tiny relatives, the plankton of the sea, are providing most of the oxygen on which our lives depend. From one-celled specks of life to the giant kelps, living in fresh and salt water, arctic snow and near-boiling hot springs, algae are among the hardiest and most widespread of living things, and the most ancient. Probably the first life on earth was a one-celled alga, and the germ plasm you carry in your reproductive organs has been inherited in an unbroken line of descent from this first self-replicating protein of the primeval sea.

CALIFORNIA SAGEBRUSH is shown here in its late summer and winter aspect, with dry spent stalks of summer bloom.

As you walk along the trail above China Cove you'll pass a dead Monterey pine. It's easy to see the **CONES** still attached to the trunk of the tree, having started out on a small branch and persisting as the branch grew into a thick trunk.

Behind the rocks and trees of the cove rise the **SANTA LUCIA MOUNTAINS**. Viscaino, the Spaniard, saw them rising straight out of the sea south of here as he sailed up the coast toward the Bay of Monterey in 1602. It happened to be St. Lucy's Day, December 13, and the mountains still carry the name he gave them. They say if you pick a budding branch of a flowering tree on St. Lucy's Day and put it in a vase indoors, that it will bloom on Christmas Day.

Along the trail between China Cove and Bird Island you will be sure to see the golden **CALIFORNIA POPPY** anytime in spring or summer. The poppy was "discovered", meaning seen and described by a western European person, by Luis Née, who, with Thaddeus Haenke were the first botanists to make collections in California and accompanied Malaspina on a Spanish scientific expedition in 1791. The next year, 1792, Menzies, the Scots botanist sailing with Vancouver on a British voyage on the California coast, collected the flower, which mouldered on herbarium sheets in England without ever being named, while the seeds he sent to the Royal Botanical Garden at Kew sprouted "weakling plants which perished without issue". The Russians sent out their voyage of exploration round the world in 1816 and 1823, commanded by Kotzebue, with Adelbert Chamisso, a Frenchman, as naturalist, and of course he noticed the poppy, collected it, and named it after his friend and fellow naturalist on the voyage, Johann Friedrich Eschscholtz, and today the genus is called _Eschscholzia_. This mouthful of consonants lost a "t" somewhere during its journey from California to Europe and into the scientific literature. Now the plant is cultivated round the world.

The lizard you see disappearing into the bushes as you disturb its sunbath is probably the **WESTERN FENCE LIZARD**, common in warm places all over California. Gray-brown camouflage on the back turns to bright blue and yellow blotches on the underside, which the male lizard displays to other lizards as a warning to keep off his territory, in an ominous-looking up and down dance of push-ups.

1 the golden flower
California Poppy
Eschscholzia californica

2 the lizard
Western Fence Lizard
Sceloporous occidentalis

Look in the kelp offshore as you walk along the edge of the cliff past Gibson Beach; you'll often see a **GREAT BLUE HERON**, a large wading bird, seeming to be miraculously walking on water. The heron is standing on a floating log or on the kelp itself, spearing small fish just as it does when standing in a shallow pond. The blue-gray bird stands four feet high.

This is a good place to look for **SEA OTTERS** also. Listen first, you can sometimes hear the tap-tap of an otter breaking a shellfish on a rock. One of the rare tool-using animals, the otter has learned to dive for a rock and for a sea urchin or mussel at the same time. Then, floating on its back and balancing the rock on its chest, the otter pounds the hard shell on the rock until the shell breaks. Tucking the rock under one foreleg, the otter may use it again after diving for more food. Crabs and some other prey are eaten without cracking. After eating, the otter rolls round and round in the water, cleaning its fur of debris. Otters do not have a layer of blubber that keeps them warm in the cold Pacific water as the sea lions and whales do; they depend on their thick rich fur to hold an insulating air layer near the skin. The price of that thick fur almost caused the otter's extinction by the 1850's; now our laws protect them. Otters are probably born in the water and live most of their lives in the sea. To rest they often drape kelp around themselves and sleep belly up on the water, securely anchored from drifting. They hold their paws out of the water to conserve body heat. Although otters are commonly seen from San Luis Obispo county to Santa Cruz county, there may be only 1600 animals altogether. One oil spill in Monterey Bay could destroy almost the entire species.

1 the large blue-gray bird
Great Blue Heron
Ardea _herodias_

2 the brown floats
Bull Kelp
Nereocystis _luetkiana_

3 the yellowish-brown kelp
Giant Kelp
Macrocystis _pyrifera_

4 the mammal
Sea Otter
Enhydra _lutris_

1. the black birds
   Cormorants
   Phalacrocorax sp.

2. the gray-green bush
   Bush lupine
   Lupinus arboreus

3. the yellow flowers
   Lizard-Tail Yarrow
   Eriophyllum staechadifolium

4. the white flowers
   Yarrow
   Achillea borealis

5 the soaring birds
Brown Pelican
Pelecanus occidentalis

6 the tall plant
Bee Plant
Scrophularia californica

7 the golden poppy
California Poppy
Eschscholzia californica

THE BIRD ISLAND TRAIL

After a good rainy winter this sun flooded spot can be a dazzling flower garden in spring. Above the flowers rise the white barren slopes of **BIRD ISLAND**, and if it is a hot day with a sea breeze from the west you can smell right away what the white frosting on the rocks is. Nesting on the island in spring and summer are Brandt's and Pelagic Cormorants and some Western Gulls. You may see a few Brown Pelicans flying by, but they no longer nest here. Harbor Seals may be basking on the rocks near the water, and some Sea Lions will probably be talking loudly a little higher on the rocks. All animals living in the Reserve are fully protected. There are few places where wild animals have allowed us to share so closely the cycles of their lives. Interfering with the animals' lives in any way betrays their trust in us.

The tallest, rankly growing flowering plant in the middle of the garden is **BEE PLANT**. The flowers are not conspicuous, being little dark reddish brown jugs. The plant is in a family called Scrophulariaceae a wonderful word to roll off your tongue, and referring to Scrophula, a loathsome disease involving glandular swellings, as all the plants in the family show characteristic glands.

The tall heavy head of small white flowers growing above soft fern-like aromatic foliage is **YARROW**. The dried

stalks of a related species in China were used for div-
ination; a handful of a certain number of stalks were
thrown, and how they fell referred the diviner to a pas-
sage in the I Ching, or Book of Changes, a Taoist text.

The granite cliffs account for the very **CLEAR WATER**
in these coves and inlets. No sediment or crumbling rock
clouds the water. The granodiorite rock slowly wears
away into the brilliant white sand of China Cove and
Gibson Beach. This sand has a very low iron content
and produces a pure white glass, used for optics and
laboratory glass. Dunes of similar sand were mined
from Asilomar Beach, on the western end of the Monterey peninsula.

The **RESERVE CLOSES** about an hour before sunset.
If you are annoyed that you cannot watch the sunset
from the rocks of the point, know that the dusky hours of
sunset, and also those of dawn, are the hours when most
animals come out to forage or hunt. Deer from the mountains cross the highway and browse the bushes, bobcats
come out to hunt foraging rabbits, and the mountain lion is
occasionally seen. To have a few hundred people wandering in the Reserve at these hours would disrupt the feeding of the animals.

1 the nesting birds
Brandt's Cormorant
Phalacrocorax penicillatus

2 the dignified birds
Brown Pelicans
Pelecanus occidentalis

3 the gulls
Western Gull
Larus occidentalis

4 the smaller cormorant
Pelagic Cormorant
Phalacrocorax pelagicus

THE BIRD ISLAND TRAIL

Here is a close-up view of Bird Island in case you do not have binoculars. The many black birds nesting here in spring and summer are **BRANDT'S CORMORANTS.** During the breeding season they show a bright blue throat, not easy to see. Nesting on the exposed cliff faces on the rocks around Bird Island are **PELAGIC CORMORANTS,** who have white flank patches in spring. Cormorants do not have waterproof plumage; their feathers get wet. They hang around the rocks most of the time, entering the water only to fish. They swim very low in the water, sometimes with only the head and neck rising above the surface, then, with a little leap forward, they dive headfirst underwater after fish. When they come out of the water, they extend their wings to dry in the sun and wind, as you are sure to see them doing. In spring you can watch the birds building shallow nests of seaweed, often stealing a shred from a nest nearby. The nests are spaced just out of reach of the neighbor's thieving bill. Cormorants are permanent residents of Point Lobos. By late summer they are finished raising young and spend the winter perched on rocks along the shore.

The large prehistoric-looking birds soaring low over the waves or standing with dignity on Bird Island are **BROWN PEL-ICANS.** They come up from their breeding grounds in Baja California and the Channel Islands off Southern California and sit on rocks and wharf pilings during the summer or fly majestically over the ocean, sometimes stoping in mid-flap to fall head first into the sea, feet trailing, as if stricken with a sudden lethal malady, but bobbing up serene as ever, guzzling a fish. Pelicans have hundreds of air sacs under the skin which buoy up their large bodies in the water. They use their gular pouches as scoops to aid in catching fish. When Jean François Galoup de la Pérouse, the commander of a French scientific expedition round the world, sailed into Monterey Bay in 1786, he noted in his journal that the bay was covered with pelicans. In the 1930's hundreds of them nested on Bird Island. The last nesting pelican noticed here was in 1960. The shrinking of the pelican population has been traced to the use of DDT and other persistent pesticides. These toxic substances flow from the agricultural fields into streams, into the ocean, are absorbed by plankton which are eaten by fish and the fish eaten by pelicans, in whom the concentrated DDT indirectly causes the shells of their eggs to become so thin they collapse when incubated. Since widespread use of these pesticides has been banned, the birds now are able successfully to hatch young. Pelicans are now thought of as a threatened species. They are making a slow recovery, but their fate may still be uncertain.

Eight species of gulls can be seen at Point Lobos; **WESTERN GULLS** are the most common and the only species to nest here. Different species of gulls are hard to tell apart. Western gulls have a dark gray mantle and wings, flesh colored legs and a yellow bill. Immature gulls of most species are a mottled brown and white. Gulls are scavengers and will pick up just about anything remotely edible, dead or alive, that they can find along the beaches and rocks of the seashore. They pick over low tide rocks for small sea life and steal fish from pelicans and other birds if they can. You may see gulls floating near a feeding otter, snatching scraps.

SOME BOOKS

these books are specific to Point Lobos

Frincke and Terry, Birds of Point Lobos, Sacramento, State of
  California Department of Parks and Recreation. black and white.

Legg and Wilson, Point Lobos Wildflowers, Sacramento, State
  of California Department of Parks and Recreation, 1954. color.

Point Lobos State Reserve, Interpretation of a Primitive Landscape, Aubrey Drury, ed., Sacramento, State of California
  Department of Parks and Recreation, 1954. black and white.

most bookstores carry these field guides. Their color pictures
make them good companions to this book in your hand.

Peterson Field Guide Series, Boston, Houghton Mifflin Co.
  Excellent illustrations in these guides to birds, mammals, fish, etc.

Audubon Field Guide Series, New York, Alfred Knopf.
  color photographs of birds, mammals, trees, flowers, insects, etc.

California Natural History Guides, Berkeley, University of
  California Press. Guides to flowers, mammals, butterflies, trees,
  seashore life, etc. Specific to Northern or Southern California.

Munz, Philip. California Spring Wildflowers, 1961, Shore Wildflowers of California, Oregon and Washington, 1964, and more.
  Berkeley, University of California Press.

these books are about marine life.

Gotshall and Laurent, _Pacific Subtidal Invertebrates_, Los Osos, Sea Challengers, 1979. Brilliant color photographs.

Scheffer, _A Natural History of Marine Mammals_, New York, Charles Scribner's Sons. 1976

———

these books are interesting and/or entertaining.

Coats, Alice, _The Plant Hunters_, New York, McGraw-Hill, 1970

Graustein, _Thomas Nuttall, Naturalist_, Harvard University Press, 1967

Greenwalt, _Hummingbirds_, New York, Doubleday, 1960

Kingdon-Ward, _The Romance of Plant Hunting_, London, 1924

Merriam, C. Hart, _Dawn of the World_, Arthur Clark Co, 1910. California Indian tales about plants and animals.

Morwood, _Traveler in a Vanished Landscape_, Clarkson + Potter, 1973. biography of David Douglas.

Saunders, _Western Wildflowers and their Stories_, New York, Doubleday, 1933

Stejneger, _Georg Wilhelm Steller_, Harvard University Press, 1970

Walker, _Seacoast of Bohemia_, Peregrine Smith, 1973. Early Carmel days.

the journals of Explorers and Naturalists such as Vancouver, Galoup de la Pérouse, Lewis and Clark, Beechey, Menzies, Coulter, etc., can be found in libraries and make history real.

ABOUT THE ARTIST/AUTHOR

Frances Thompson discovered that she got the best results painting the final plates for this book by sitting right down in the dirt of the trails at Point Lobos with her drawing board, paper, ink, inkstone, water and brushes. She apologizes to the many passers-by who wanted to talk with her there, but found her smiling around a pencil clutched between her teeth, saying nothing. She studies classical Chinese brush painting with Alison Stilwell Cameron, who studied with masters in China. She lived three years in the Ventana Wilderness near Monterey at Tassajara Zen Mountain Center, practicing Zen with masters Shunryo Suzuki and Ryogen Tatsugami. She worked as a biological illustrator in San Francisco, New York and Los Angeles. She completed a degree in graphic art at the University of California at Los Angeles, and returned there for three years of graduate work in zoology and botany. Her only literary qualification is having won a short story contest in a horse magazine at age 12. She was born in Japan. She lives near Monterey.

She continues her lifelong wandering among the mountains and lowlands, deserts and waters, creatures and growing plants living on the earth from the Rocky Mountains to the Pacific, carrying her drawing board in her pack and drawing what she sees there.

ACKNOWLEDGMENTS

From the first moment this book flashed, complete, into my mind, until several years later, when it appeared, complete, in my hand, everyone involved in its production has been unfailingly supportive. Pat Hughes, chairperson of the Point Lobos Natural History Assc., and Ranger Rod Parsons have been ever helpful since I presented them the idea. The Point Lobos Natural History Assc. assisted the publication of the book with a $2,500 interest-free loan, read the manuscript several times and gave helpful recommendations. Judson Vandevere patiently answered questions, reviewed the manuscript and wrote the descriptive foreword. Fran Ciesla proofread over and over and made the useful index. Morton Tenenbaum did literary editing. Norine Haven picked out the last errors. The Pacific Grove, Monterey and Carmel Public Libraries gave invaluable service. Their Interlibrary Loan Service provided books from all over the state. Leslie Navari, Reference Librarian at the Pacific Grove Public Library, was especially helpful, as were Alan Baldridge and Susan Harris of the Hopkins Marine Station Library, and Vern Yadon of the Pacific Grove Museum of Natural History. Lorri Lockwood typed the first readable manuscript. Ethyl Hart kept me to my agreement to complete the art when I said I would. Robert Wirtz, of Curriculum Development Assc., Monterey, gave of his knowledge of printing and bookmaking. Frank Gamberutti, of Instant Type, Monterey, shot the line work. Kira Godbe pasted it on pages. Harry Timmins, of Gallery Graphics, Carmel, handled with skill the art reproduction, printing and manufacturing of the book, gave apt recommendations and was all-around helpful and encouraging. Much appreciation goes to the following people for their financial assistance to the book and to the Point Lobos Natural History Assc. — Robert and Pat Evans, Rev. David Hill, Donald and Kitty Ide, John Joyner, Ralf Kahl, Monica Martin, David Moody, Margaret Owings, Dave Shonman, Jo Stallard, Jean and Morton Tenenbaum, Minnie Tenenbaum and Jack and Marion Wisberg. Alison Stilwell Cameron empowered my heart and hand to undertake this project.

INDEX
underlined numbers refer to illustrations